1.98

POSTERS *AT THE TURN OF THE CENTURY*

POSTERS

AT THE TURN OF THE CENTURY

Maurice Rickards

WALKER AND COMPANY, NEW YORK

First published in the United States of America in 1968 by Walker and Company, a division of the Walker Publishing Company, Inc.

Published simultaneously in Canada by The Ryerson Press, Toronto.

Library of Congress Catalog Card Number: 68–22132.

Printed and bound in Great Britain.

List of Illustrations

The Turn of the Century

It is as well to remember that the Turn of the Century is a figment of the mind—a mathematical concept only. History takes no account of it. Nor does the solar system. As the world rolls from one century into another the moment of transition is imperceptible; neither in the cosmos nor in the affairs of man is there a seam to show where the centuries join.

Historians make a special point of this. They warn us to avoid the temptation of dealing with periods of history as though they had been marked, if not with seams, then with punctuation marks —measured into convenient portions for ease of future reference. But all the same we must admit that there is a certain magic about the Turn of the Century, even if it is all in the mind. Certainly for our forebears in 1899 there was. It appeared almost as though history had become aware of numbers; there were great things afoot.

The last few years had been full of excitement; there had been Herr Diesel with his patent for a petrol engine and Benz with an actual four-wheel vehicle; Edison had opened his Kinetoscope Parlor in New York and the Lumière Brothers had come up with the Cinematographe; the last volume of *Das Kapital* had appeared, so had *The Time Machine* and so had a strange work called *Studien über Hysterie* by S. Freud. There was talk of a machine for setting printer's type and a machine for recording sound. There was even talk of a flying machine. In 1899 the Dortmund-Ems Canal was opened. Aspirin was invented. At The Hague there was a 26-nation Peace Conference to extend the Geneva Convention to naval warfare, to explosive bullets and poison gas, and to set up a Permanent Court of Arbitration. Everything was happening.

The new year kept up the pace. So did its successors. In rapid succession there was the first transmission of speech by radio, the first zeppelin flight, Max Planck with his Quantum business;

S. Freud again with *The Interpretation of Dreams and The Psychopathology of Everyday Life*; somebody called Heaviside with his layer and Bayliss and Starling with something called hormones. There was the theory of radioactivity, the photo-electric cell, the ultra-violet lamp, safety razor blades, the founding of a company called Rolls-Royce, and in New York the opening of the Broadway Subway, with electric trains from City Hall. In 1905 the first neon signs appeared, the first motor-buses came to London, and in Germany an unusually complicated theory was propounded by the Director of the Kaiser Wilhelm Institute for Physics, Professor A. Einstein.

This was the jumping, swinging, with-it world of the Turn of the Century, breathless with the pace of progress, avid for more. It was remarkable. And like any other random sample of history, it abounded with anachronism. There was the usual co-existence of yesterday and tomorrow, the overlap of generations. It saw the death of Verdi and the birth of Disney; the death of Gauguin and the birth of Dietrich; the death of Johann Strauss, of Gladstone and Chekhov, and the birth of C. P. Snow and of Shostakovich. It saw the wood engraving and flash photography, the horse bus and internal combustion; lamp oil, acetylene, gas mantles and the New Electric Bulbs.

There were people who could clearly remember meeting Charles Dickens. Garibaldi, Balzac, the Duke of Wellington, Daudet, Schopenhauer—these were names of only yesterday. If you were exceptionally lucky you might have shaken hands with both Goethe and T. S. Eliot. It was a crazy mixed-up wonderful age.

It was also the age of the coming of the poster. As industry gathered momentum, as paper and print got cheaper, as the new world of mass production broke in on the tempo of the old, the poster spattered out across Europe. And here again there was the

overlap effect; almost without realising what was happening the 'fine' artist, the dedicated velvet-jacketed artist of tradition, was seduced. There was a new gallery for him, out in the open air.

In Paris they took the art of the poster seriously. Chéret, master of the poster for more than a decade before Toulouse-Lautrec moved in, was a household name all over France. They say that before he finished he produced nearly a thousand designs; his work was known and watched for as keenly by the connoisseur as by the crossing sweeper. But Toulouse-Lautrec brought something new to the poster; Chéret himself said so.

Lautrec's posters were so striking that people wanted not only to look at them but to possess them. Bill-stickers did a brisk black-market trade in supplying enthusiasts at the side door; people who could not afford black-market prices waited until the poster was pasted up and the bill-sticker had gone, and carefully peeled it off before the paste was dry. It was with Lautrec's work that the poster-collecting habit really started, and—with his posters certainly—it has never really stopped.

What was the secret of his appeal? How was it that this trundling little dwarf, this brothel-fancier—how was it that he made so unmistakable and so lasting a mark? His first colour lithograph, a poster for the newly opened *Moulin Rouge*, caused an immediate sensation. By contrast with the subtler tints of Chéret it was crude and garish. It attracted notice not only by the vigour of its style. It must be conceded that there was the matter of the scandalously dazzling knee-length drawers of *La Goulue*, heroine of the piece. But this was no *succès de scandale*; it was clear that to The Poster—and certainly to Paris—something had happened.

Lautrec had turned to the poster because he had found it difficult to get a showing for his ordinary lithographs. Almost accidentally and almost overnight a new idiom was born. It was an idiom that was to be taken up around the world. Lautrec owed

Moulin Rouge Bal Masqué 1891 (France) *Henri Toulouse-Lautrec*

9

much to the background of his early years; he was an admirer of his contemporaries, Dégas, Manet, Vuillard and Bonnard. But as they had influenced him, now it was his turn to influence others; for perhaps a quarter of a century to come, perhaps longer, his spirit was to move in the world of graphic design.

A contemporary was Steinlen. No brotheliser, and by no means eccentric, Steinlen still had the touch of Lautrec. His poster for Nestlé's Milk could scarcely be further in subject from the *Moulin Rouge*, but there is the same authoritative simplicity, the same bold impact. Some say that Steinlen copied Lautrec. Others say the other way about. Others say that they influenced each other, interacting and complementary. Whatever it was, between them they formed the power drive of something very big. Edgar Penfield and Will Bradley in America moved into gear with it. So, with his own contribution, did Aubrey Beardsley. Somewhere along the line came Alfons Maria Mucha, ultimate expression of the whole remarkable thing. They called it *l'art nouveau*.

What was the secret of Lautrec? Nobody really knew. Not even S. Freud. There are mysterious forces operating in society; like measles or chicken pox they incubate, unseen; suddenly, as though at some secret signal, they break out—everywhere at once. Now that we see it with hindsight it seems that Toulouse-Lautrec was part of a wider thing, part of the Wilde-Lautrec-Beardsley syndrome. (The *Echo de Paris* reported that the applause of the first-night audience at the Paris performance of Wilde's *Salome*—to which Lautrec had contributed a programme lithograph—'rang across the channel, through the English prison walls to reach the unfortunate prisoner in Reading Gaol'.)

Lautrec, like all his brother poster artists, found himself working for an odd variety of clients. There were the obvious ones, like the revues, the clubs and restaurants and publishers, and there were

Nestlé's Milk c. 1892 (France) *Théophile Steinlen*

10

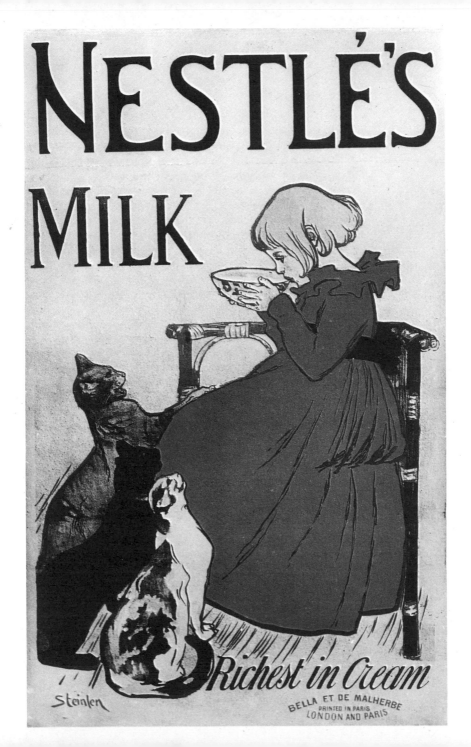

the clearly unexpected ones, like the London confetti manufacturer (113 Charing Cross Road), the Place Pigalle photographer
and—perhaps least advisedly of all—a manufacturer of bicycle
chains. There was even at one time talk of a poster for Job, the
cigarette paper people. It must be said that in the department of
bicycle chains Lautrec was not in his element. One sees, in his
straying from his own territory, an almost ludicrous misapplication;
we are embarrassed for him.

But industry rolled on around the artist inexorably. No-one
could declare himself exempt from its demands; Mucha, recipient
of honours, Chevalier of the Order of Francis Joseph I, Officier of
the Legion d'Honneur, designed posters not only for Sarah
Bernhardt but, as Brian Reade tells us, posters for the champagne
firm of Ruinart, and the printing firms of Lorilleux and Cassan Fils;
advertisements of tooth-paste, bath tablets, cigarette papers,
chocolates, Waverley Cycles, Nestlé's Food for Infants, and much
else. 'In fact he made two posters for this last firm, one in English,
and also a large horizontal one to celebrate the Diamond Jubilee
with three portraits of Queen Victoria in roundels, over the words
Hommage Respectueux de Nestlé.'

It was about this time that posters—and indeed advertising in
general—began to enter the dangerous age. As well as being
striking and attractive there was a requirement that it should be
slightly misleading. The *Electricine* poster is typical of the white
lies that commerce could not resist; with gas well established and
electricity just around the corner, the status-rating of the oil lamp
had slipped; what better means to brighten up business than a
lamp oil called *Electricine*? No doubt M. Lefevre pondered the
point as he did the drawing. But he got away with it more con-
vincingly than did Lautrec with his bicycle chains.

Back across the Channel, as well as Reading Gaol there was

Electricine 1895 (France) *L. Lefevre*

12

Windsor Castle and the security of the British way of life. Arthur Pearson was founding the *Daily Express* and there was a new dance called the cake-walk. Ladysmith and Mafeking had been relieved. Apart from Bertrand Russell's newly published *Critical Exposition of the Philosophy of Leibniz*, everything appeared to be still all right.

At Olympia, London's sensational new centre for large-scale exhibitions and musical spectaculars, Mr Edwin Cleary was cashing in on the glories of Empire. In an extravaganza which he entitled, *Briton, Boer and Black*—but which the show itself extended to cover 'an actual Eskimo encampment'—dominion was depicted not only over palm and pine, but igloo too. Dudley Hardy's poster was appropriately non-committal. The official programme featured a varied list of attractions showing 'episodes in the life, chase and warfare from the Cape to Cairo . . . showing the subjects of Her Majesty from the northernmost to the southernmost points of the British Empire.' The show had a cast of hundreds; there were 'actual Soudanese', Zulus, Ashantis. There were performing elephants and African baboons. There were also '40 real Eskimos, 14 real Eskimo dog teams, 2 real arctic igloos and 12 Eskimo harpooners'. It was a major presentation. The public was advised however that 'the items were subject to frequent alterations'. Extracts from the published synopsis of Scene IV suggest that casualties may have been heavy: *Officer calls for volunteer to take down the Boer Flag—Trooper succeeds in doing so . . . Loud whistle of armoured train, which dashes on—Truck opens, revealing Naval Brigade and Maxim guns—Guns detrained and mounted—Heavy firing and repeated hand-to-hand struggles between Boers and British, culminating in final victory for our arms . . .*

There was also the Royal Biorama—'the largest living pictures ever shown'. These included a panoramic view of Capetown with Table Mountain in the distance and the landing place of our troops.

Olympia 1900 (Britain) *Dudley Hardy*

14

Also 'one of the great troopships surging through the water on her way to South Africa', and 'President Kruger leaving his residence and stepping into his carriage to be driven to the Volkesraad'. Other pictures would be given, said the programme, 'from time to time as they arrived from the seat of war'.

It was to be only a dozen or so years before the Olympia arena was housing genuine prisoners of war from Germany.

If big-scale show-business was getting under way, so was the use of the big-scale poster. The poster had become bigger—and noticeably bolder; it was still only precariously under control. Still firmly rooted in the piratical tradition of free-for-all flyposting, it had a fine disregard for authority; it spread in a proliferation almost to the point of plague. It was true that there was no longer the anarchy of physical violence (fly-posting competition had escalated almost into gang-warfare in the earlier part of the century) but the scale and drive of the thing had got badly out of hand.

The 70s, 80s and 90s brought a burgeoning of poster hoardings all over the world. These, many of them two or even three storeys high, were the new 'respectable' medium of public proclamation. Instead of battling with each other for unofficial space on house sides, street lamps, and any other unoccupied surface, bill-stickers had taken to setting up on their own as hoarding contractors. They prospered; but they also defaced a lot of town and countryside. One of them, Alexander Scott of South London, put up a gigantic hoarding in Trafalgar Square. This, 'The External Paper-Hanging Station', was a highspot in an unbroken record of excess.

Any centre of tourist attraction, any natural beauty spot, was fair game for the external paper hangers. Holiday resorts, lakes, rivers—even the fjords of the Arctic Circle, blossomed with the slogans of Victorian enterprise. The Thousand Islands of the St Lawrence River carried stove polish and tooth powder slogans. The Mississippi, the Hudson River and the Rocks of the Nevada Canyons all received the attention of this 'dynamic new industry'.

Pears' Soap   c. 1895 (Britain) *Harry Furniss*

It was inevitable that the community should take protective action. In South Africa there was an outcry when it was proposed that the face of Table Mountain be used as the world's biggest billboard. There was a narrow escape for Niagara Falls when the authorities only just managed to ban a similar project there; in Britain things came to a head with two hoardings put up by an American firm of food manufacturers on the White Cliffs of Dover. These are reputed to have weighed eight tons and to have been visible from France. It took the Society for the Checking of Abuses in Public Advertising (since canonised as the Advisory Council for the Control of Outdoor Advertising), the Mayor and Corporation of Dover, and a Parliamentary Bill in Her Majesty's House of Commons to get them taken down again.

This was the Awful Golden Age of advertising; the initiative lay heavily with the poster men; the law had not the imagination to anticipate the direction from which the next inroad would come.

Typical of the ebullience of the age was Pears' 'Dear Sir' poster. It had a double, if not a triple, twist. Thomas Barratt, publicity whiz-kid, 'Father of Modern Advertising' and director of Pears, persuaded Lillie Langtry to endorse his soap with the words: *Since using Pears' Soap I have discarded all others*. A thief copied her signature from the advertisement and withdrew all her jewels from her bank. He got away with £40,000-worth. With the words of the endorsement still fresh in the public mind, *Punch* published its 'tramp' version, which in turn Thomas Barratt acquired and exploited as a poster. It achieved a fame immeasurably greater than the Langtry original. It also did much to break down public resistance to advertising.

As Wildhack's poster for Scribner's elegantly shows, the motor car too was making its inroads; internal combustion was beginning to acquire overtones not only of science but of status. And unlike Lautrec with his bicycles, Wildhack was able to cope with the newcomer. The Scribner's design perfectly integrated the handling of elements which, up to that time, had been regarded as incompatible.

Scribner's c. 1906 (USA) *Robert J. Wildhack*

Apart from their essential simplicity of treatment neither the poster for Pears nor the one for Olympia was in the mainstream of the design movement of the period. Nor of course did they make any concession to the advent of internal combustion. Their subjects made no demands of up-to-dateness—indeed it was almost a requirement that they should stay where they were—firmly and safely in the nineteenth century. Harry Furniss's drawing for Pears was not originally conceived as a poster; its happy adaptation to use on the hoardings is a piece of straightforward good luck, typical of the Midas touch that often goes with the adaptomania of the inspired amateur. Dudley Hardy's Boer War hero constitutes a poster only in the stark abstraction of the figure from its background. The style and treatment of the figure itself is in direct line of succession not from the *Moulin Rouge*, but from the *Monarch of the Glen*. Lautrec has left no mark here. Neither has Beardsley or any of the strange new crowd. In Liverpool however, notwithstanding the absence of motor cars, they were thinking what Manchester and London were to think tomorrow.

The Sefton Restaurant poster takes note not only of the Henri/Aubrey axis, but of Mucha himself. Reserved and anglo-saxon as it is, it bears the authentic stamp of the world of its day. Like almost every other poster from Amsterdam to Omaha, Lewis Baumer's design has the statutory ingredients; here is the rhythmic tangle of the lady's hair, the fulsome figure within its tenuous outline, the curlicues and lettering fancywork.

In comparing this poster with the Mucha over the page, one significant difference is worth noting; whereas the figure in the Liverpool job is crowded out with an overload of lettering—the ratio between figure and lettering is about fifty-fifty—in the Mucha poster the girl gets unmistakable pride of place. Regardless of the relative merits of the artists in question, the visual impact of the Adelphi Hotel suffers from its surfeit of words. It may be judged

Adelphi Hotel, Liverpool   c. 1895 (Britain) *Lewis Baumer*

how strong this poster might have been if the lettering around the figure of the girl is masked out, enlarging the figure to fill almost the whole of the poster. A Mucha would have contrived the inclusion of most of the lettering in panels above and below the figure; the rest of it he would have persuaded the management of the Adelphi Hotel to omit as unnecessary.

It has often been said that the English are on the whole suspicious of pictures, whereas they feel perfectly at home with words. Perhaps this accounts for their tendency to include both elements in their posters and, to be on the safe side, in more or less equal quantities.

On Boxing Day 1894 the artist Alfons Mucha happened to be correcting proofs in the offices of Lemercier et Cie, the printers. The telephone rang. The director of Lemercier was called. The voice on the phone was that of the director of the Théâtre de la Renaissance; could anybody be found to do a design job in a hurry, he wanted to know. It was a matter of a poster for the new Sarah Bernhardt play; the man who was to have done it was ill. It was a classic situation. Mucha, without the slightest idea that immortality awaited him, looked up as the printer put down the receiver. 'You are going round to the Théâtre de la Renaissance,' he said. Mucha went.

Afterwards in a neighbouring café, he sketched out his idea for the poster as the printer watched. Unenthusiastically M. de Brunhoff agreed that Mucha should go to the second stage—of a full-size colour drawing on canvas. Sarah Bernhardt was a woman of no little character; her decisions were dramatic, and final. She saw the design and fell for it immediately. In what must have been one of the quickest poster production jobs on record, Mucha immediately transferred the design on to the printing stones; within five days of the original phone call the poster was printed and delivered.

For Mucha this was very much more than just an assignment in

JOB Cigarette Papers 1896 (France) *Alfons Mucha*

22

a hurry. It was to turn into a full-time job. Sarah Bernhardt signed him up on a six-year contract; he was to design all her posters henceforth, and all the other bits and pieces of printed matter that the Bernhardt image required. There were also stage sets and costumes. Mucha had arrived with a bang.

But he was never entirely sold on the 'commercial' art that this work involved. In the years of success that followed, he fought a battle with his own mounting dissatisfaction and the unending tides of additional work that the Sarah Bernhardt *cachet* produced. In the end he came to reject it all.

His poster work relied heavily on the almost magic appeal of his individual vision and his preoccupation with the full-size female form. Whatever his posters advertised there was little risk of his women being swallowed by the advertiser's message. As in the case of the Job cigarette-paper poster the product was always an also-ran; he seems to have utilised his poster commissions as vehicles for the working out of some inner compulsion rather than as exercises in public persuasion. It may legitimately be asked just how many packets of Job cigarette papers did the Mucha poster actually sell. Or were the advertisers content with the public relations value of the reflection of the Mucha glory?

One may wonder what he would have made of the Barnum and Bailey assignment—and what, if he had undertaken it, his clients would have thought of it—and what, if they had accepted it, it would have sold in the way of circus tickets. Of one thing we may be sure: whatever the aesthetics of the anonymous poster we see here, it certainly pulled in the cash customers.

1896, like most of the 'nineties, was a good year for a mixed bag. Puccini finished *La Bohème*, The Nobel Prizes were set up, Chekhov's *The Seagull* had its first performance, the *Daily Mail* appeared for the first time (a halfpenny) and somewhere in the south of England Herbert George Wells was writing *The Invisible*

Barnum & Bailey 1893 (USA) *Anonymous*

24

Man. It was a good year for electricity too. The first electrified main-line railway had just opened, Marconi had demonstrated wireless telegraphy, in France they were building an electric submarine, and Rutherford was tinkering with the magnetic detection of wireless waves. In more than one capital they were building— or thinking of building—electric railways. Under the exalted patronage of His Majesty King William II, Stuttgart was showing the world an exhibition of electrics and applied arts.

The exhibition poster sums up the predicament of the time. Here unmistakably is the overlap of epochs in uneasy co-existence. The worried-looking angel, trapped uncomfortably between the millstones of time, is clearly doubtful of the wisdom of it all. (There is some danger, surely, in this harnessing of the sky's lightning? Is it safe to serve like this, as an *ad hoc* fuse-wire between the power and the wheel?)

The artist has taken refuge in the familiar idiom of the public monument. The winged figures, the heroic postures, the pedestals and laurels of classic mythology had always come to the rescue in the hour of allegory; here, reliably, they came again. How else, after all, could you convey the mysteries of a voltaic battery? This poster has its own genealogy and its own idiom. It was to be only a few years later that its idiom returned in full force; in 1914, in every one of the belligerent languages, posters appeared with their winged victories, their guardian angels and declamatory figures—the whole dramatis personae of classical allegory. They formed a supranational heavenly army, fighting for everybody.

The Stuttgart angel, at this early stage uncertain equally of her role and of the engineering viability of the partially-flanged railway wheel, soon got used to her job. She was to be much in demand, particularly in transport advertising, for the next two or three decades. Portentous as the times undoubtedly were—with

Exhibition of Electrotechnics and Applied Arts, Stuttgart 1896 (Germany) *TK*

technology busting out all over and angels working overtime, we must not forget that these were also the Naughty Nineties. In Paris, particularly, there had been a revival in the public appreciation of sex. The *Moulin Rouge*, the *Théâtre du Rire*, the raucous night-shows with their gaslight flares and froth of lingerie—these were the haunts not only of paunchy businessmen and goggle-eyed provincials: it was here that Toulouse-Lautrec and his cronies sought Nirvana, here that gathered the avant-garde of artistic and literary Paris. But by the turn of the century, when Lautrec was shambling round the town, a broken and incoherent alcoholic, the spontaneous magic that had earlier been the city's saving grace wore off.

In the guttersnipe arrogance of *La Goulue*—whose décolletage descended to her navel, and whose outrageous underwear was the talk of Paris—there had been a certain extravagant integrity. In the self-conscious naughtiness that came out of it, there was not. The expression 'fin de siècle' acquired overtones of a contrived and organised wrongdoing. (It is a matter of purely parenthetic interest that during these ten or so years the gas flares that they had started out with had given place to Electric Lamps...)

Fin de Siècle, the illustrated literary journal, sought to crystallise a mood that had by this time become a shade too aware of itself. But the obliteration of a portion of its poster girl was no mere circulation gimmick. Here, to the irritation of one and all, the Censor had stepped in. Choubrac, the artist, reluctantly modified the plates (*This part of the drawing has been banned*) and retaliated by printing at his own expense a poster offering fig-leaves for sale. The Censor was unamused when it appeared on the hoardings.

In one form or another, sex was not absent from posters for long; perhaps the coming of the bicycle—itself the most sex-conscious mechanical device to date—was part of the naughty-ninety

Fin de Siècle (Illustrated Literary Journal) c. 1898 (France) *Alfred Choubrac*

FIN DE SIÈCLE

10 cmes.
le Numéro.

CETTE PARTIE DU DESSIN a été INTERDITE

Journal littéraire illustré

FIN DE SIÈCLE PUBLIE

DES ROMANS, CONTES, CHANSONS, NOUVELLES

de MM.

Paul ARÈNE	Hugues LE ROUX
Emile BERGERAT	GUY de MAUPASSANT
Ferdinand BLOCH	A. MÉNARD
Paul BONNETAIN	O. MÉTÉNIER
Paul BOURGET	Jean RICHEPIN
A. BRUANT	SAPHO
Léon CLADEL	Aurélien SCHOLL
Alphonse DAUDET	L. XANROF
René EMERY	Emile ZOLA
Edmond LEPELLETIER	Etc., etc.

GRANDS DESSINS PAR P. BALLURIAU

PARAÎT Tous les MERCREDIS ET SAMEDIS

business too. A business it certainly was—at that time mostly British. There was no doubt about its impact.

In the Whitworth poster, designed and printed in Paris by the English company's General Agent, the cycle itself is clearly male; equally clearly there are overtones of impending emancipation.

The bicycle, even though it had been around in one form or another since 1815, up to now had failed to make the grade. Only the hardiest of inveterate outdoor types could stand its rigours. Even the introduction of refinements like pedals and chain and ball bearings—even, indeed, solid rubber tyres had failed to persuade the ordinary man. But in 1888 Mr Dunlop had come up with his *inflated* tyres—'pneumatics', as they were called. This put a different complexion on the whole thing. With the addition of a gadget for free-wheeling, a Sturmey-Archer for going uphill and a Brake for going down, the bike was a going concern. The ordinary man got on and rode away.

For the ladies, however, there was a problem.

It was solved, first by the adoption of the very sensible suggestion of Amelia Bloomer (who had first thought of it some forty or fifty years before) and later by attention to the crossbar. At this stage there was a glut of bicycle posters; bloomered or not, as the particular model required, women were portrayed on bicycles in all directions at once. The prophets who had written it off as a fad 'like tennis and flying machines' were confounded.

The cycle in the Whitworth poster is of an early vintage. It has neither bell nor brake, nor lamp nor pump. It has no 3-speed and almost certainly no free-wheel. It is interesting to speculate that Kaiser Wilhelm II or Alphonse Daudet or *La Goulue*—or even Sarah Bernhardt—might have ridden it.

Another pastime that was destined to contribute its share of posters in the years ahead was the life-size animated picture. It

Whitworth Cycles c. 1890 (France) *Jean Paléologue*

30

suffered from no crossbar drawbacks and required neither skill nor courage. Better than that, it offered to young gentlemen and their young ladies the luxury of a privacy they had never known before. Both optically and socially it was an enormous success. It was, as the posters said, 'a great treat'. If it was not merely the privacy that you went for; it was also 'the sight of a lifetime'. You could see not only the China and Boer Wars but—irresistible if you lived in Birmingham—actual reproductions of life in Birmingham. Let the exclamation marks speak for themselves.

The poster for this Continuing Enormous Success at the Curzon Hall embodies a production trick that was to become standard poster practice in many fields; the main body of the poster, excluding the lettering on the screen, was printed in quantities large enough to reduce its unit cost to a minimum. The local matter, added afterwards to the requirement of (in this case) Birmingham was cheaply overprinted by a local round-the-corner printer. In this way the Curzon Hall life-size picture-show had the advantage of a slap-up artist-designed poster at a price it could afford. This accounts for the London address in the panel in the bottom left-hand corner and the strangely inconsistent perspective of the wording on the screen relative to the screen itself.

In a design that is otherwise remarkably restrained the profusion of exclamation marks is the first sign of the shape of things to come; the cinema poster—indeed cinema promotion at large— was to move into superlatives in a way that Barnum and Bailey had only toyed with. The moving picture was initially promoted in terms of scientific novelty rather than of entertainment; we see the cinema here in the last few moments before it went supercolossal, when the main headline was not the subject, but still the thrill of 'animated pictures'.

Already the pattern was established: there was a 'main feature' and a 'supporting feature'; there were scheduled times of screening and there was a graduated price range. (There was also the

Edison's Animated Pictures c. 1901 (Britain) *A. Morrow*

slightest touch of misrepresentation: the auditorium of the Curzon Hall was not, as the drawing suggests, sloped to allow you to see over the people in front. But in the excitement who would notice?)

In 1898 engineers began to drive a tunnel between Brigue in Switzerland and Iselle in the Val di Vedro in Italy. It was designed to avoid the hazards of the Simplon Pass and to open up direct rail communication between the two countries. It was to be the longest tunnel in the world. The rail trip through it today takes roughly thirty minutes. To cut the tunnel, it took Swiss and Italian engineers eight years. Between the beginning of the job and the official opening in 1906 the world had changed dramatically. In a very real sense the story of the Simplon Tunnel lies at the heart of the turn of the century; its $12\frac{1}{2}$ miles are a monument not only to the men who made it—and to the men who died making it—but to the age that conceived it.

The poster for the inaugural exhibition in Milan is frankly a flight of fancy. It is in the 'monumental' idiom of allegory; it makes no concession to the literal-minded. *(What are they doing, crouched naked on the front of the locomotive? Why a red light on the front of the train? What is the wiggle in the track in the middle distance there?)* But as a dramatic summation of the whole remarkable achievement, as an epitome of the drama of the tunnellers' years of struggle, and their ultimate success, the poster packs a notable punch.

In style it is as far from Beardsley (over the page) as it is from our hero of Olympia. It conveys its message strictly in its own idiom. Again, we may wonder what Chéret would have made of it—or Toulouse-Lautrec—or one of our later Kauffers or Henrions?

Inauguration of the Simplon Tunnel; International Exhibition
1906 (Italy) *L. Metlicovitz*

34

INAUGURATION DU TUNNEL DU SIMPLON
EXPOSITION INTERNATIONALE
MILAN = 1906
AVRIL = NOVEMBRE

There is the conviction that for all its 'oddness' it does superbly well as it stands.

Among the changes that the world had seen in the tunnel years was the disappearance of a whole harvest of famous names. It really was the end of an age: Nietzsche, Ruskin, Gladstone, Bismarck, Johann Strauss, Verdi, Zola, Whistler, Gauguin, Dvorák —they had gone down, it seemed, like ninepins. Oscar O'Flahertie Wills Wilde had gone too. So had Lautrec. So had Her Majesty the Queen, Empress of India, Defender of the Faith. Mr Aubrey Beardsley, graduate of Brighton Grammar School, consumptive, fetishist, sometime accountant in the Guardian Life Insurance Company, had preceded them all—at the age of 25—in 1898. But the drawings that he did lived after him.

If *fin-de siècle* had ever been an empty phrase, Beardsley filled it right up. With his erotic grotesquery, his tuberculous capacity for a fine, punctilious decadence, he ushered out the century in a sensuous shiver. He left school in 1888. Ten years later he was dead. But nothing was ever to be quite the same again.

Like other artists of his time he could not stand altogether aside from the demands of commerce; unlike most, he so far despised the society that suffered him that he allowed his mockery to invade his work; more often than not his assignments in illustration and decoration carried him off in flights of irrelevant rudery; he was compulsive, abstruse, and rapturously sick. His growing notoriety brought embarrassment to those who had supported him at the beginning. Even Oscar, at one stage his patron and admirer, came to view him as rather more than a joke.

One wonders how wise the publisher was to use a Beardsley drawing to grace his children's book list. *Topsys and Turvys, The Brownies Around the World, Tom Sawyer* and *The Jungle Stories* go oddly with the armchair voluptuary that flanks them. Like the Animated Pictures poster, the design was produced as a general-purpose setpiece for overprinting as occasion required. But even

'Publisher' c. 1894 (Britain) *Aubrey Beardsley*

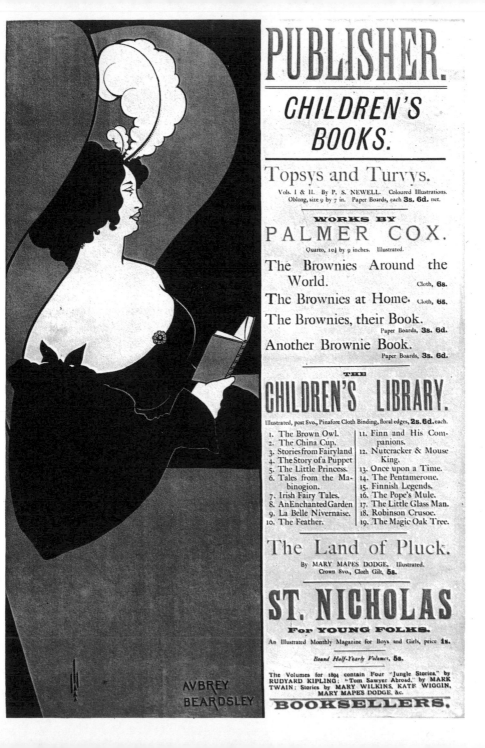

PUBLISHER.

CHILDREN'S BOOKS.

Topsys and Turvys.

Vols. I & II. By P. S. NEWELL. Coloured Illustrations.
Oblong, size 9 by 7 in. Paper Boards, each 3s. 6d. net.

WORKS BY
PALMER COX.

Quarto, 10½ by 9 inches. Illustrated.

The Brownies Around the
World. Cloth, 6s.

The Brownies at Home. Cloth, 6s.

The Brownies, their Book.

Paper Boards, 3s. 6d.

Another Brownie Book.

Paper Boards, 3s. 6d.

THE
CHILDREN'S LIBRARY.

Illustrated, post 8vo., Pinafore Cloth Binding, floral edges, 2s. 6d. each.

1. The Brown Owl.
2. The China Cup.
3. Stories from Fairyland.
4. The Story of a Puppet.
5. The Little Princess.
6. Tales from the Mabinogion.
7. Irish Fairy Tales.
8. An Enchanted Garden
9. La Belle Nivernaise.
10. The Feather.
11. Finn and His Companions.
12. Nutcracker & Mouse King.
13. Once upon a Time.
14. The Pentamerone.
15. Finnish Legends.
16. The Pope's Mule.
17. The Little Glass Man.
18. Robinson Crusoe.
19. The Magic Oak Tree.

The Land of Pluck.

By MARY MAPES DODGE. Illustrated.
Crown 8vo, Cloth Gilt, 5s.

ST. NICHOLAS

For YOUNG FOLKS.

An Illustrated Monthly Magazine for Boys and Girls, price 1s.

Bound Half-Yearly Volumes, 5s.

The Volumes for 1894 contain Four "Jungle Stories" by
RUDYARD KIPLING; "Tom Sawyer Abroad," by MARK
TWAIN; Stories by MARY WILKINS, KATE WIGGIN,
MARY MAPES DODGE, &c.

BOOKSELLERS.

AUBREY
BEARDSLEY

discounting the hazards of children's libraries, it seems doubtful that the lady was proper company for books of any kind. It is a curious sidelight on the whole Beardsley phenomenon that the transparent sensuousness—and often sinister undertones—of his creatures could by common consent be ignored. To many the Beardsley style was merely a harmless affectation to be indulged, or laughed off, according to taste.

By the healthy-minded Empire-building world at large he was mercilessly barracked. In *Punch* particularly the Aubrey Cult was held to almost weekly ridicule. Satirists went to the trouble of publishing posters signed Daubrey Weirdsley; Gilbert and Sullivan blasted him. Just as assiduously, everyone copied him. When he shortly coughed himself to death in the South of France there were Aubreys everywhere. In studios all over Europe—indeed all over the world—the contagion spread. But it never achieved the patho-logical authority of the master. In the poster for the Thanksgiving Number of the *Chap Book*, Will Bradley across the Atlantic had a gentle go at it. In posters, in chapter headings, showcards, title pieces—even in nursery motifs and Sunday School booklets—everybody had a go at it. Some seventy years later, in the turning over of the compost heap of the century that followed, people had a go at it again. Somehow it refused to be left alone.

But in the year that Beardsley died, the Curies discovered radium, the first petrol tractor was built, and the Paris Métro opened up. The world went on without him. And what the Simplon Tunnel was to do for Italy and Switzerland, the *Transport à Grande Vitesse* was doing for France and Britain.

It was Napoleon who, a hundred years before, had carved him-self a carriageway over the Alps at Simplon; it was still Napoleon's shade that haunted England every time the word 'tunnel' came up —as it often did in the Simplon period. A tunnel under the English Channel had been proposed by a Frenchman as far back as 1856.

The Chap Book Thanksgiving Number c. 1900 (USA) *William Bradley*

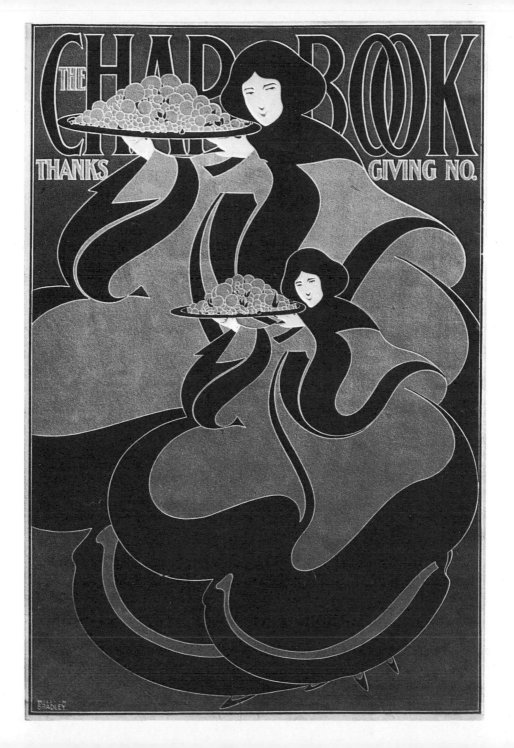

It was a frightening idea then, and it was no less frightening now. True, Gladstone had favoured it (as, perhaps not surprisingly, had Brunel and Robert Stevenson) but Joseph Chamberlain (and, perhaps not surprisingly, the War Office) had opposed it. There had been a Joint Select Committee of the House of Commons— and the War Office had won. But the year after the Simplon Tunnel opened for business Albert Sartiaux focused attention on the Channel once again with a work disturbingly entitled *Le Tunnel Sous-Marin*. The year after that Blériot did the same thing, earning himself £1000 for his trouble, by flying it.

But still there was no direct link. Not even a train ferry.

Thus it was that the improbably named *Chemins de Fer de l'Ouest et de Brighton* inaugurated its revolutionary new *Service Journalier Accéléré* for the rapid transport of flowers, fruit and vegetables overnight from the Gare St Lazare to Victoria Station, London. This was a tremendous new concept in proximity; it had the same note of luxurious daring as today's daily airlifts of asparagus or strawberries from California. *Goods deposited at St Lazare Station in time to leave by the four o'clock afternoon train will be delivered in London the following morning, first thing.* We observe the discreet avoidance of a precise arrival time; but first thing was early enough, whatever it was. Here on a station platform in the heart of London (the 'Brighton Line', of hand-bag fame) were delicacies from the foreign fields of only yesterday. The Continent was moving closer. Before very long Victoria Station was to blazon from its canopy the exciting legend *Direct Routes to Paris and All Parts of the Continent.* You could hardly get much closer than that.

The poster was a harvest festival in itself. With a final touch of informality the citizens of Paris were assured that prospective *expediteurs* who applied for detailed information would receive an explanatory folder, actually sent to them 'à domicile'.

Chemins de Fer de l'Ouest et de Brighton (Announcement of a new high-speed transport service, Paris/London, for market produce), c. 1903 (France) *Gustave Fraipont*

CHEMINS DE FER DE L'OUEST et de BRIGHTON
Fleurs, Fruits, Primeurs
à destination de LONDRES
Organisation d'un nouveau service
journalier accéléré entre
PARIS-St LAZARE & LONDRES
pour le transport des
FLEURS, FRUITS, PRIMEURS
et autres marchandises
à grande vitesse.
Les marchandises déposées
à la Gare St Lazare assez à temps
pour partir par le train de 4 heures
de l'après-midi seront livrées
à Londres le lendemain matin
à la première heure.
Les expéditeurs qui en
demande recevront à domicile un bulletin
détaillé de ce nouveau service
POUR TOUS RENSEIGNEMENTS COMPLÉMENTAIRES S'ADRESSER :
GARE St-LAZARE et Bureaux de Ville de la Compagnie
SERVICES INTERNATIONAUX 21 rue d'Amsterdam
PARIS
G. FRAIPONT

As far as the water's edge, at least, the railways of Britain were going great guns. Their expansion answered not only the demands of industry for inter-city communications and for import/export routes to the sea, there was big new business in the seaside for its own sake. There began to emerge an alliance of interests between the resorts and the various privately owned railway companies that served them. It was even rumoured in some areas that railway directors doubled up their commercial interests by investing, as well as in the tracks, in their destinations too.

It was not surprising therefore that places like Skegness came to be so bracing. John Hassall, who was to have a long and varied career on Britain's hoardings, sold his bounding fisherman to the Great Northern Railway Company for the sum of £12. It was to be used to advertise a series of Sunday excursions from King's Cross (Return fare 3/—). It put Skegness and Hassall on the map; it has been in use more or less continuously by the railways and the resort, and by their heirs, successors and assigns, ever since. It was republished by way of Jubilee in the spring of 1968.

Not since the days of George Hudson had the railways been so buoyant and so go-ahead. The first passenger train had steamed into London in 1836, the year that Dickens wrote *Pickwick Papers.* But it was not so very long after, in 1862, that they started something really new; trains in tunnels under the town. By the turn of the century the network of subterranean railways had spread so much that you could get almost anywhere as easily below as you could on top—sometimes, with the mounting tangle of hansom cabs and motor-cars on the streets, more easily.

People came to take the tube by habit. (Did not even Oscar himself, commuting to his first and only job in Fleet Street, take the Metropolitan Line every day from Sloane Square?) Apart from the noise, and the people, it was really not unpleasant at all.

The network beneath the streets grew ever outwards. Soon the

Skegness/Great Northern Railway Company 1908 (Britain) *John Hassall*

system was linking up with overground lines outside the town. It became possible to go—through a hole in the ground—far out into the countryside. It was scarcely credible. And with a population bursting at the seams (it had more than doubled the two and a quarter million of Dickens' day) it not only allowed Londoners a temporary escape; it let them take the town with them to the country. They lived out there, some of them as far as Harrow, Sudbury and Perivale.

London's transportation system, evolving over the years from the chaos of its early multiplicity to the single integrated unit of today, took to the poster early on. Its buildings and its vehicles were first-class poster sites for anybody. Within the gigantic poster industry that it helped to spawn, it loomed large. Sometimes, to the other advertisers whose posters flanked it cheek by jowl, it served as a foil; sometimes as a shining example, sometimes as a relief. But that was in maturity. In 1907, when the poster for the Underground carried its customers Right into the Heart of the Country, life in the transport business was still real, earnest and commercial. This was strictly a poster for business. With the fresh air and the fields at hand, with its sober load of middle-class respectability—and with obviously room for plenty more—the District Railway carriage in the picture had an inescapable appeal.

This, before it got slick and sophisticated, and before publicity men had learnt to omit unnecessary full stops and commas, and before lettering had become an occupation for gentlemen, this was the genuine early London Transport article. It was hard-selling, idyllicised, naive, literal and slightly misleading; it stands midway between yesterday's Lautrec and Kauffer still to come. It stands unconsciously close to the Archduke Ferdinand and the pointing finger of Kitchener. Only seven years from now there were to be customers sleeping on the platforms at the Elephant and Castle, sheltering as the zeppelins came over.

In later years the London Transport poster was to occupy an

London Electric Railway Co. 1908 (Britain) *Anonymous*

enviable position; where its friends and neighbours were committed to persuasion, London Transport merely sought to please; it was burdened with no imperative of sales response and it conveyed no message more complex than a greeting to the traveller on his way. In this simple capacity it achieved world-wide fame. In its heyday—with a clientele that threatened to overwhelm it with business, it was more truly a wall decoration than a poster. It was eventually to reach a stage where it provided patronage to artists—visibility to the unknown, and the occasional holiday for the known. To many it served as a cornerstone for a poster collection.

At the turn of the century the poster had come out of the trial and error stage; it had settled down to an idiom that was generally understood. There was still the overlap of styles—new graphic fashions side by side with old—but for the most part the public had come to accept it as a feature of the daily landscape. What had not yet settled down was agreement among advertisers as to what was a subject for a poster and what was not. The media research men had not been born. If bicycles had posters, why not sauce, or coffee, or corsets?

George Fasoli and Son, Venetian corset manufacturers, had little doubt of the pulling power of a *buon busto* for only 5 lire. Their crypto-Beardsley girl (or was she neo-Lautrec?) was very high fashion indeed and the deftness of the presentation of the product was at the same time decent, striking and amusing. But was it through the medium of the public poster—almost literally in the market place—that you sold a woman a corset? There were doubts.

The economic structure of an industry and its means of distribution governs the mode and extent of its advertising. So does the

Fasoli, Fabbrica Busti; (*The Good Corset 5 lire*), c. 1898 (Italy) *Anonymous*

nature of the product and the nature of the consumer. The turn of the century offered only three main channels of approach to the public. One was the press, another was posters, and the third was putting up hoardings on the cliffs of Dover. The last, for most advertisers, was out. Between posters and press there was indecision. Clearly it was only the big-market product that could really stand the strain of costly poster campaigns. Equally clearly there were products that were better suited to the relative intimacy of the newspaper.

For a long spell there was confusion; quite often manufacturers would publish posters for no more cogent reason than the thrill of seeing the company name in the public eye. (The same thing still happens occasionally today, where a publicity manager sees to it that the Chairman's route home has at least one hoarding to his credit.) Other manufacturers would go into posters on a try-it-and-see basis. It was a costly game.

If we are puzzled by posters advertising products that the economics of today would prohibit, we must bear in mind the still-experimental marketing techniques of the time. *Huile Russe*, the Belgian shoe preparation for ladies, might just make out on poster promotion. Or it might not. Apart from the disaster that will surely occur when she knocks the bottle over, as we view the poster we are subconsciously concerned for the economics of the thing. But seen strictly from the front of the house, this is a superbly effective design. Its unassuming simplicity of treatment, and its complete freedom from idyllicism, give it an impact and a credibility rare in advertising—now, or then. Whereas the figures in the carriage on the District Railway have reality without conviction, whereas the Job cigarette-paper girl has conviction without reality, the petticoated girl on the kitchen chair is guaranteed genuine human being—one of us—no nonsense and no kidding. But her reality is

Huile Russe (Shoe cream), c. 1896 (Belgium) *Rassenfosse*

A. BÉNARD . LIÉGE

HUILE RUSSE

H. PIRON - Rue Bara, 46, BRUXELLES

PRIX DU FLACON
1f 50

not at the cost of sensitivity. The drawing has delicacy of line, subtlety of tone and a graphic integrity all its own.

The proprietors of the Imprimerie Camis are not over-concerned with credibility. Apart from their natural desire to show us how well they print posters—and how big, and artistic, they are—they show heavy reliance on our suspension of disbelief. Like the poster of the lightning-conducting Stuttgart angel, this is a poster in the grand tradition of monumentality. From somewhere, one feels, there should come the sound of celestial choirs. How triumphal the arch, how luscious the all-too-fleshly beckoning guardian angel, how vast the Works, how gigantic the *plus grandes machines du monde.* If anyone has ever entertained doubts about the scale and calibre of Camis the Printers, he may shed them now. Through these portals must surely pass the most distinguished customers in the world.

And yet it must be said that the hundreds of them actually doing so in the picture have a curiously insubstantial look; certainly they have less reality than the girl on the door. One suspects that they are an afterthought, drawn in by another hand (after who knows what ructions) at the behest of some city-slicker sales director.

Are they *really* customers? Their uncertain merging into the masonry and their apparent ingestion into the production line is full of a haunting ambiguity. Was it perhaps just an Open Day . . . ? Comparison of the detailed mosaic-work on the lettered architrave with the careless rendering of the crowd (not to mention its collectively odd perspective) confirms the view that something went wrong. But quand-même, what a poster.

The heroic style, the grand allegorical setpiece, is a bloom that has always flourished better in the soil of the south; to the more literal anglo-saxon mind its acceptance needs a conscious intellectual effort. The view that a spade is implacably a spade has little

Camis, Printers (*The biggest machines in the world; Posters, Pictures, Calendars, Albums, Gravure, Chromo*). c. 1899 (France) *Anonymous*

room for the amateur dramatics of allegory. Except for emergencies like actual warfare, the girl on top of the Old Bailey, and perhaps Britannia and the Statue of Liberty, is about as far as you need to go.

It is like opera. To the anglo-saxon there is something faintly embarrassing in conversation sung in English; the same applies to the impact of visual allegory. But by a curious metamorphosis, once removed from the anglo-saxon context, both become more or less acceptable. Perhaps it is a fault of the context; perhaps of the flight of fancy; wherever the fault lies, it is a fact that *La Bohème* seems far more sensible in Italian. The *Birra Italia* poster does too. It is only necessary to make a mental substitution of the words *Birra Italia—Milano* for *Worthington—Burton-on-Trent* to make the point inescapable.

But given its context, given its time, no matter how spade the anglo-saxon spade, this is a poster of very high enchantment. It is true that it enjoys the same unfair privilege of London Transport, the same freedom from 'hard sell'. It has no complicated message to convey; it attempts no twist of the arm, no bang on the head. It demands of itself nothing more than a greeting to the traveller in passing—a reminder of the existence of a world of fantasy that is absolutely real. In its evocation of elysium, of sweetness and light and joyful liberality—surely there can never have been a poster so four-square out of this world. Skilfully avoiding any risk of indelicacy, Hohenstein's naked ladies *float* in attendance. For all its edenly overtones—to say nothing of its hint of a *ménage à trois*—the poster is free of even the breath of actual scandal; the indisputably off-ground touch of the ladies is assurance enough of the decencies. (We observe the care with which Hohenstein has outlined the legs and feet of the girl on the right; she really is walking on air . . .) At whichever level the customers view it, on

Birra Italia   c. 1898 (Italy)   *Hohenstein*

or off the ground, this is truly a poster for the gods. Could the beer be anything but the same?

From its earliest years, in fact since posters had first attracted the notice of the orthodox artist, there had been controversy about the true role of fine art in poster advertising. The distinction—even in the minds of the 'poster painters'—was often uncertain. Was not a poster merely a picture with words put in? It must be conceded that the *Birra Italia* poster was a not-too-remotely-distant relative of some of the gigantic canvasses of Rubens and Van Dyke, with their bacchanalian setpieces and their groups of woodland maidens roistering round Silenus. The treatment is more modest, but the genealogy is clear.

Many advertisers, not bothering about the niceties of the fitness of things, went straight to the fine arts and used them—with the simple addition of the appropriate wording—as they stood. Sir John Millais, for example, whose ill-fated bubble-blowing grandson was to find his unofficial way to the hoardings, was livid. But there was nothing he could do about it. It was none other than Thomas Barratt, of Lillie-Langtry-used-no-other fame, who hijacked the painting; he did so perfectly legitimately, buying the painting for £2300 from Sir William Ingram of the *Illustrated London News* (who had himself planned to use it as a give-away colour plate in his magazine) and conferring upon it an unexpected twist of immortality. Although Millais was eventually mollified— it was after all very good publicity for him—there were many who believed that his reputation suffered fatal damage.

But there were artists who needed no hijacking. Whatever their private reservations, they moved in with a will. There was Lautrec, for a start. There was Mucha; there was Steinlen. Then there was the remarkable case of Nicholson and Pryde.

These two men, both of them 'fine' artists, each with a style and a reputation in his own right, each with a promising career in front

Pears' Soap c. 1889 (Britain) *Sir John Everett Millais*

of him, met as brothers-in-law. There is still some uncertainty about just what it was that pushed them into posters — a field of which neither of them had more than a passing knowledge. Nor is very much known about the exact part that each played in the partnership. But for an intensive spell from 1894 to 1895 they combined, as the Beggarstaff Brothers, to produce a series of posters that are now known throughout the world.

In a converted public-house, the *Eight Bells* at Denham, they jointly worked; they evolved a poster technique of quite exceptional power. Without clients, and without briefing other than their own common sense, they devised designs for hypothetical advertisers; they worked all hours of the day and night, cutting and pasting coloured paper in the simplest possible lines and shapes. By some alchemy there emerged the expression of a corporate personality.

Nothing like it had been seen before. Ruthlessly simple, and yet charged with a maximum of character and sensitivity, the Beggarstaff designs made a huge impact. For a public nurtured on posters in a more 'arty' style, they took a lot of getting used to. Some raved. Some did not.

The output of the partnership was limited. Where, in the Hall of Poster Immortality, Chéret had more than a thousand posters, where Lautrec had thirty, the Beggarstaffs had barely a dozen. In terms of revenue the whole enterprise was a failure. For their most celebrated design, the poster for Irving's production of *Don Quixote* at the Lyceum, which was to become perhaps the most famous poster of all time, they asked £50. Irving gave them £100. But as fate had it, the poster never actually appeared; *Don Quixote* was a flop.

The Beggarstaff story is one of the strangest in the history of graphics. With a name that one of them took from a sack found lying in a Denham outhouse, there came into being ·a fully-rounded individual; for each of them this separate personality was

Don Quixote 1895 (Britain)
Beggarstaff Brothers (James Pryde and William Nicholson)

a shared projection. They had, as it were, a joint *alter ego*. 'I have become,' wrote Pryde to a friend, 'half a poster artist.'

We see the Beggarstaffs during their brief collaboration, busy by oil-lamp in their converted pub, in the daytime trailing round potential clients with enormous rolls of paper on which their cut-out designs were pasted. Their poster for Rowntree's Elect Cocoa (also to become a classic) first made its appearance in the Rowntree offices as a fifteen-foot roll of paper carried in between them. We see them, on one memorable occasion at Denham, hand-producing not merely the original drawing for a poster, but the actual run of the full-size stencilled job—a poster they had designed for a Hereford production of *Hamlet*.

When, through lack of funds, the partnership ended, they moved back, each to his own ground, to become painters once more. Each achieved a comfortable distinction. But it seems not unlikely that the Beggarstaffs will outlive them.

Technology had galloped ahead. As well as the introduction of Rowntree's special new Elect Cocoa, there had been the Armour Company's special new extract of meat in Paris. Less sensitive about the disposition of lines and masses, the Armour people had jumped right in at the French end with a poster printed in the temple of printing technology, the Imprimerie Camis. The shake-up that was to follow the U.S. federal investigation into conditions in American stockyards was yet to come.

Also yet to come was the full impact of electricity. But the gas people were already beginning to get nervous. There was a mounting threat of obsolescence. Since the beginning of the century, gas had been the very latest thing. With ever-increasing brightness the flicker of gas had lit not only the streets, the theatres and

Armour & Company *(The only extract to preserve the flavour of the fresh meat).*
c. 1896 (France) *Anonymous*

buildings but, so it seemed, the century itself. By the beginning of the 1880s the hiss of gas was everywhere. Then, just when all had been set for a life of gaslit ease, the new Electric Lamps had come in. So when Von Welsbach came up with his marvellous new light intensifier—the Gas Mantle—the industry breathed again; there was a respite.

The poster for jets and mantles epitomises the moment; apart from its claims for a fifty-per-cent saving and four times the light (and apart from the engaging candour of the salesgirl's garment) the poster has a number of points of interest.

We observe not only the gas-mantled light with its halo of sparkling brightness, not only the conventional street lamp with its fishtail flame; there is more. A closer look reveals that the decorative tangle that frames the picture is composed of gas-piping; the lower section is the very gas main itself; above, concealed in the *art nouveau* curlicues in the top right-hand corner, is a multi-flame burner; along the top appears a camouflaged array of fishtail jets. There is still more: the sunflower clasped in the girl's left hand is a space heater, the petalled flames of which are keeping the poor girl warm. Nothing has been overlooked; here is the very model of go-ahead gas graphics; in the long history of lost causes, surely there was never a more glorious final throw than this. Here, not content with as comprehensive a pictorial rendering as ever gas got, not content with facts, figures and the very latest in technology, we have a see-through dress and toplessness all in one. How could it fail?

There is one point unresolved: the small print at the foot of the cartouche in this Belgian poster reads (in *Italian*) Executed in the Italian Cartographic Institute, Rome. We may be forgiven if the point gives rise to speculation. What possible link could there be

The "Auer" Gas Burner (*50% Economy—4 Times the Light*) c. 1897 (Belgium) *U. Cleman*

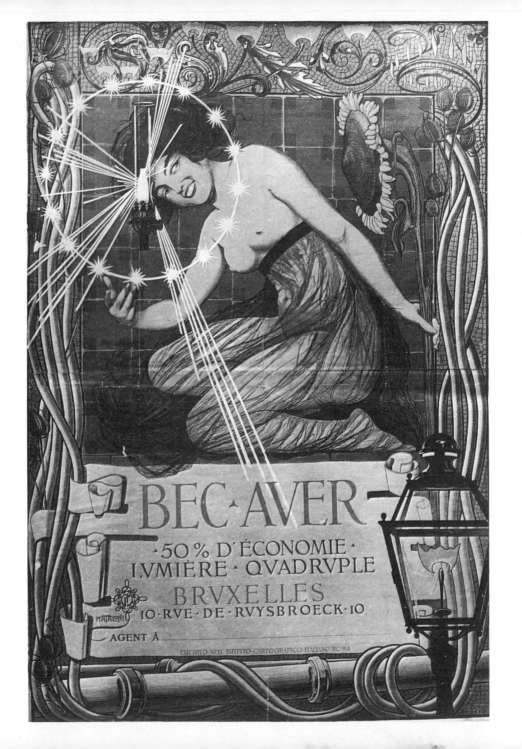

between Belgian gas and Italian maps? And that dress—
cartographic?

More primly topless, perhaps, was Robert Fowler's autumn girl
for the Walker Art Gallery. If the naughty nineties of the Continent
had brought a sometimes startling permissiveness to posters, in
England there were still decided reservations. Exposure of the
female form, whether in posters, sculpture or any other medium,
was confined strictly to the figures of mythology or to the
indisputably finer arts, such as *September Morn* and *Love Locked
Out.*

It was identification with both these categories that must have
excused the *déshabillé* of the doomy young woman with the mahl-
stick. Had she been advertising anything in the world but an art
exhibition the police authorities would undoubtedly have run her
in. Even as it is, it seems very unlikely that Sir Andrew Walker (to
whose open-handedness the gallery owed its existence) would
have approved. In addition to the matter of the lady's dress, there
is about the poster more than a touch of the old Aubrey. Is it our
imagination, or is there something slightly sinister in the *mise en
scène*—some nameless secret that unites its figures and its bits
and pieces? What is the owl doing in the picture? And what is the
meaning of the smirking thing on the left—harmlessly pedestalled,
it is true, but still manifestly up to no good? We wonder, as Sir
Andrew would have done, what strange circumstances could have
brought them all together—she without brushes to her pallette,
the pedestal with its sprouting branches . . . But we observe the
obvious innocence of the poster's punctuation, we remember the
weight of the gallery's load of Rodins, Whistlers and Watts's, and
we give it the benefit of the doubt.

Clothed or otherwise, the female figure has always been a useful
poster standby—from autumn art to Barnum and Bailey, from
bicycles to beer, from gas to O.K. Sauce. Poster artists have

Walker Art Gallery Autumn Exhibition c. 1903 (Britain) *Robert Fowler*

invoked her from the start. Take Chéret for example. Among the thousand or so posters that he produced, it is safe to say that 988 of them featured women. Chéret may be said to have invented, if not the pin-up, certainly the paste-up. Unlike Robert Fowler's brooding girl, Chéret's confections were a froth of hilarity and light. At a time when the fly-posted streets of Paris were suffering the rough edge of the tongue of authority, the posters of Chéret were enthusiastically defended all the way round. His ice-rink poster is typical. He brought to every subject the same successful formula; he created the 'Chéret girl'—and he made her sell everything that came his way.

Inveighing against the drabness and ugliness of Paris (and against M. Alphond, Director of the Board of Public Works) one writer speaks for all Paris in welcome of Chéret: 'He has a very personal and Parisian point of view, which is at once superficial, charming and adorably false. He sees wings, as it were, in the glamour of theatrical fairyland. In the essence of Paris, which he distills, he leaves aside the horrid dregs, neglects the acrid and corrosive sourness, and perceives only the effervescence, the bubbles floating to the surface. He gives us a delicate intoxication of sparkling wine, an *ivresse* of a rosy exhalation. He personifies it in his women, charming in their glowing and smiling abandon. He takes a girl of the people, mischievous-looking, with eyes which flash and sparkle. He refines her, makes her seem almost distinguished in her tinsel, gives her the air of a soubrette of other days whose very frailties excuse themselves by their very delicacy.'

It will be seen that Chéret was more than a poster artist; he was a national institution. As Englishmen speak of cricket, Frenchmen spoke of Chéret—with a glow of feeling amounting in unguarded moments to a lump in the throat.

But although he was still going strong at the turn of the century (he was a man of sixty when he did the Palais de Glace poster in

Palais de Glace 1896 (France) *Jules Chéret*

64

1896) his beginnings were firmly rooted in the France of the 1700s. He knew nothing of *art nouveau* and the shape of things to come. Born in 1836, his admiration was for the paintings of the eighteenth century. He did his first poster (in black and white) in 1855. It was after a spell in London, where he learnt the techniques of colour lithography, that he moved in on the world of the colour poster. It was thus towards the end of his career that Toulouse-Lautrec and the new mood of the turn of the century took over. And when Chéret acclaimed Lautrec as his successor—as he did, publicly, in 1892—it was not a succession in direct line of descent. Chéret was the end of a line; Lautrec was a new one altogether. They both knew it. But Lautrec was greatly touched by Chéret's declaration; he counted it such an honour, so the story goes, that he had himself photographed raising his hat to a Chéret poster.

Chéret lived to be 96. Full of honours, and full of the nineteenth century, he died at Nice in 1932.

France was the poster growth-spot at the turn of the century. But it must not be concluded that all was either Palais de Glace or Moulin Rouge. Just as there were large areas of British graphics that remained immune, both to the old-style Chéret *panache* and to the blast of *art nouveau*, so France had its blind spots. The posters published from 17 rue de Maubeuge existed in a world of their own. They are typical of a twilight genre, an idiom that had its beginnings not on the hoardings but on the labels and cartons of pharmaceuticals. The gathering tide of cures and nostrums brought its own design conventions. Expressions like *Elixir* and *No More Epidemics* (both favoured at the rue Maubeuge) were common ingredients. It was an idiom that was to die hard—even to be artificially regenerated in the production-line days when these products were being bought out by big industry. The stability and reliability conveyed by the 'old fashioned' look was to become a selling point worth preserving.

But the advertisers with truly big-scale vision moved into the twentieth century without a backward glance; they were like men

Parfumerie Orientale c. 1896 (France) *Jean Paléologue*

possessed. Hudson's Soap, using all the promotion tricks that we know today, gave away children's books, blotting pads, grocers' billheads, menu cards, pin-cases—and a coloured pin-up of W. G. Grace in flannels whiter than sunlight. They used ex-government military observation balloons for publicity flights; they hired fleets of advertising horse buses; they were among the first in the field with gift coupons. William Lever, king of Sunlight, exchanged 25,000 soap wrappers for an actual motor car. At Geneva, on two specially chartered lake steamers, he organised a washerwoman's washing contest—*La Fête des Blanchisseuses*: the world's newspapers reported it. In Britain, in the days when French ten-centime pieces circulated as freely as pennies, Thomas Barrett imported a quarter of a million of them and stamped the word *Pears* on every one of them. As giveaways they were cheap at the price.

Mason's, the O.K. Sauce people, were not far behind. With the background support of a campaign slogan (*Saucy, but quite O.K.*) they published the *O.K. Fox Trot*, a minor classic in the emerging popular style. The sheet music cover featured a scantily dressed young woman—also in the emerging popular style—the campaign slogan, the title of the song, and the words TWO SHILLINGS. As well as publicity, Mason's clearly expected actual revenue. With unassailable logic, the back cover carried the addendum *If you like the O.K. Fox Trot, try the O.K. Sauce.* The new century, well into its stride, was really swinging.

But in the final resolution the promotion gimmick rested on the support of the day-to-day poster. The giveaways and gas balloons were merely highspots in the continuing process of persuasion. The respectably dressed girl in the Mason's poster (here only very discreetly Saucy) was the long-term image that the company relied on. It was as a girl on a poster, not a girl in a song, that she sold the most sauce.

From the design standpoint the O.K. poster links the centuries.

Mason's O.K. Sauce c. 1909 (Britain) *Anonymous*

It bears the unmistakable mark of the 1890s and the unmistakable mark of the day after tomorrow—the looming 1920s. In its broad masses, its decisive outlines, its simplicity and economy, it has something of the best of both worlds. She is still, identifiably, a Chéret girl. But any day now she will be demanding the vote.

At the turn of the century the poster came into its own. It was still evolving, still experimental, but it had sorted itself into distinct evolutionary channels. Not everywhere did it move at the same pace. Cross-fertilisation was quickest on the continent of Europe, less so at the periphery. Britain and Scandinavia were slow. In America the big billboards of the major advertisers were still in their early stages; the greatest accent fell on the small 'window bills' of the magazine advertisers; these, in an intellectual climate more favourable to their reception, sold themselves to their readers on the work of men like Penfield, Bradley, Edwards, J. J. Gould, Maxfield Parrish and Will Carqueville. Here there was a discernible link with the way things were going in Europe.

Penfield's poster for Harper's February issue is typical of a whole string of designs, often produced in six- or twelve-monthly series by a single designer. *Scribner's The Century, Harper's International, Lipincott's, The Bookman* and *Chap Book*—these and a handful of other magazines made room for a big new wave in graphic design.

Like most of the Chérets and Muchas, the Steinlens and the Lautrecs, many of these posters are today collectors' pieces.

As indeed is the Turn of the Century itself.

Harper's c. 1900 (USA) *Edgar Penfield*

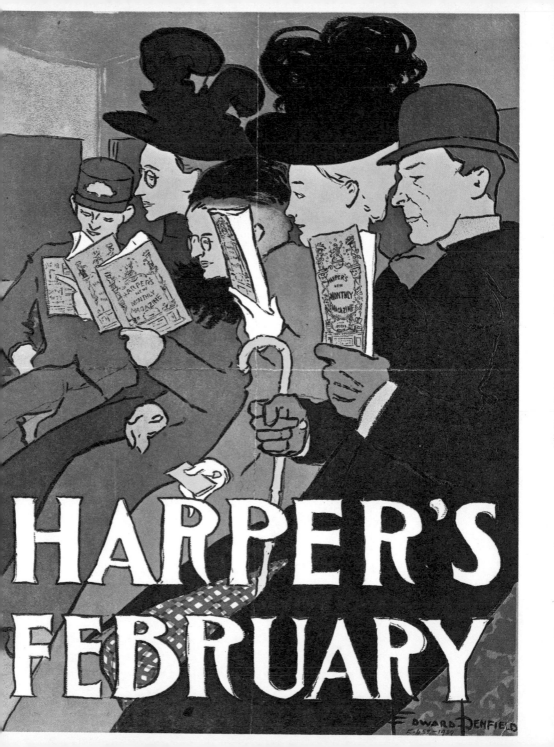

Acknowledgements

Among the many organizations and individuals who have helped in the preparation of this book, the author and publisher would especially like to thank the staff of the Print Room of the Victoria and Albert Museum, and Gibbs Proprietaries Ltd (Pears), London Transport, George Mason Ltd (OK Sauce), Olympia Exhibitions Ltd and Skegness Urban District Council.